MARGARET THATCHER

The Iron Lady

Written by Sébastien Porcu
Translated by Jessica Foster

History 50MINUTES.com

MARGARET THATCHER

KEY INFORMATION

- **Born:** 13 October 1925 in Grantham (Lincolnshire).
- **Died:** 8 April 2013 in London.
- **Political party:** the Conservative Party.
- **Main achievements:** Thatcherism (name given to the economic and political measures taken by Margaret Thatcher) and the United Kingdom's economic recovery.

INTRODUCTION

Idolised by some, condemned by others, Margaret Thatcher was a key political figure of the 20th century. Known for her shock declarations, her bushy hair and her pearl earrings, she was described by François Mitterand (French statesman, 1916-1996) as having "the mouth of Marilyn Monroe and the eyes of Caligula".

British Prime Minister from 1979 to 1990, she was the first woman to hold the position and to keep it for such a long time. Nicknamed the Iron Lady following her 1976 speech against the Soviet Union, Margaret Thatcher demonstrated a fierce inflexibility and unusual stubbornness throughout her career. At the same time, she implemented strict economic policies, which are more commonly known as Thatcherism. They included the privatisation of state-owned companies, limiting the power of trade unions and lower taxation for higher incomes. These measures were certainly favourable to economic growth, but on a social level were catastrophic. Two events in particularly stand out for this controversial figure: the hunger strike by Irish Republicans (March 1981), aborted after 172 days because of Thatcher's unfazed silence, and the Falklands War (April-June 1982), which ensured her a political victory but is also sadly remembered for its heavy death toll. But who really was Margaret Thatcher?

BIOGRAPHY

Portrait of Margaret Thatcher, dated 1983.

A STRICT UPBRINGING

Margaret Hilda Roberts was born on 13 October 1925 in her father's small grocery in Grantham. Throughout her life, she would admire this man for his personal success, which he owed only to himself. Thanks to his teaching, she learned perseverance, a refusal to quit and integrity. She had, howe-ver, a very different relationship with her mother, Beatrice. Alongside her older sister, she had a childhood structured around Methodism, piano lessons, private schools and Sunday church services.

METHODISM

Methodism is a religious movement that began in England in the 18th century with the preacher and theologian John Wesley (1703-1791). Devotion to Christianity, doing good deeds and preaching the good news are its key principles.

THE BEGINNINGS OF A VOCATION

It was thanks to her father that Thatcher became interested in politics. He in fact became a local councillor in 1936, and his main aim was defending small businesses. As his campaign resonated with the general public, he was elected mayor of Grantham in 1945. In the meantime, the young girl focused on her studies and gained a scholarship to Somerville College, Oxford, where she earned a degree in chemistry. Curious and eager to learn, she was particularly struck by Friedrich Hayek's book *The Road to Serfdom*, which was based on economic neoliberalism, something she would get many of her ideas from.

FROM HER POLITICAL BEGINNINGS TO THE CREATION OF AN ICON

Thatcher entered Parliament in 1959, the year the Conservatives returned to power. These favourable circumstances led her to gain the position of Education Secretary in 1970. Her moment of glory arrived when she replaced Edward Heath (1916-2005) as leader of the Conservative Party in 1975. She progressed and caused a stir within her own party when she questioned some of its main principles: indulging trade unions, Europhilia (a favourable view of the European Union) and egalitarianism.

Photo of Margaret Thatcher in September 1975.

On 19 January 1976, Thatcher spoke in London. She gave a damning speech against the Soviet Union and communism, which was gradually spreading. According to her, the Russians "put guns before butter". Following this famous, cutting speech about the USSR, the media started referring to her as the Iron Lady. An icon was born.

FROM THATCHERISM TO THE FALKLANDS WAR

Elected Prime Minister in 1979, Thatcher was the first woman to hold this title. She began her economic plans by demanding a reduction in Britain's contribution to Europe, a demand that would be met due to her fierce determination. She also implemented her policy of deflation to strengthen the pound sterling.

In March 1981, she was put to the test for the first time: Bobby Sands (1954-1981), an Irish republican prisoner, and his comrades began a hunger strike in order to obtain the status of political prisoners, thus showing their desire to receive better treatment. But the Iron Lady remained unmoved and ignored their request. Bobby Sands died on 5 May during the hunger strike and nine other prisoners would also die this way shortly afterwards. The strike ended after 172 days.

Subsequently, Thatcher's popularity diminished in the polls due to her political positions. In order to fix this, she decided to make the sovereignty of the Falkland Islands her hobby-horse. These Southern Atlantic islands in fact represented a strategic point as they constituted an opening to Antarctica, which had not yet been explored. The Iron Lady then launched an impressive offensive to win them back, to the great displeasure of the Argentinians, in April 1982. The fight was extremely deadly, as 905 people lost their lives, including 255 British people.

FROM PRIVATISATION TO HER RESIGNATION

Thatcher's victory in the Falklands ensured her re-election and brought the Conservatives one of their best results yet. In the wake of this success, Thatcher decided to privatise 29 public companies, thus considerably weakening the state. This measure nonetheless boosted the economy: indeed, privatising a business forced the new owners to implement profitable management strategies, which was not the case with public businesses. This consequently attracted foreign investors. But Thatcher particularly contributed to the decline of the public system by downgrading the education system as well as increasing poverty and social inequality. The society that the Iron Lady created was one that favoured privilege.

The Poll Tax, a new tax that she wanted to implement, would prove fatal for her. This tax, which the working classes judged inegalitarian, caused riots. Thatcher was disowned by her party and left politics on 22 November 1990.

DECLINING HEALTH

Having retired from politics, Thatcher decided to dedicate her time to her foundation, which promoted liberalism across Europe. She also gave talks until 2002. After that, a series of strokes forced her to withdraw from public life. She would nonetheless reappear on certain occasions, for example upon the death of Ronald Reagan (American statesman, 1911-2004), who was a close friend of hers.

Thatcher died in London on 8 April 2013 following another stroke. Although her neoliberal policies had given the country its longest period of prosperity, they had also plunged the population into a social bloodbath.

Thatcher's coffin is taken to St. Paul's Cathedral, London.

CONTEXT

A DIRE ECONOMY

In the 1950s, the United Kingdom was in a poor state. Following the Second World War (1939-1945), its economic situation had become considerably worse. It was behind in comparison to other countries: its growth had not even reached 3%, while its European neighbours, such as France and Germany, were enjoying 5% growth. Since the end of the war, the state had increased its authority, partly due to the nationalisation of services and transportation, and a welfare state had been implemented in 1930. When this happened, the country's expenses became even larger, which did not exactly help the situation.

THE WELFARE STATE

This conception of the state gives it more power to intervene, particularly on economic and social levels. This way of organising society yielded more equality, as it involved wealth distribution.

HIT WHERE IT HURT

In 1973, an oil crisis led to shocking rates of inflation of up to 25%. This was truly devastating for the United Kingdom, which found itself on the verge of ruin three years later. The situation was so bad that the country had to call on the International Monetary Fund (IMF) in 1976. It is easy to imagine the country's shame at having to do this, when just a short time previously they were boasting about having a well-performing economic system. The United Kingdom was thus loaned 4 billion dollars, on the non-negotiable condition that a deflationist policy was implemented. The unions, who wanted higher salaries, thus saw their demands rejected by the government, and many strikes began across the country.

THE UNION AGAINST "RAMPANT SOCIALISM"

Faced with the considerable importance that the trade unions had taken on, Thatcher decided to base her political campaign on their "rampant socialism". The Labour Party narrowly defeated the Conservatives in the 1974 elections, winning 301 of 635 seats.

Thatcher then replaced Edward Heath as leader of the party, but remained in the opposition. Her victory was more due to an anti-trade union vote than to real approval of her economic programme. This did not stop her, once she was in office, from deciding to redouble her efforts by implementing her budget reductions, getting rid of additional fringe benefits for employees and raising banks' interest rates to reduce inflation.

THE WINTER OF DISCONTENT

In 1978-1979, the United Kingdom was the setting for some chaotic events. The trade unions held the country hostage during the famous Winter of Discontent. This expression, first used by the English playwright William Shakespeare (1564-1616) in his play *Richard III* (1592-1593), was brought back by an editor from *The Sun* newspaper to illustrate the consequences of Labour's attempt to cap salary increases at 5%.

In response to this measure, many more strikes began across the country, in every sector. There were power cuts and food shortages. In spite of themselves, the strikers ensured that Margaret Thatcher was elected to office in 10 Downing Street (the residence of the British Prime Minister). The population overwhelmingly voted Conservative and the Iron Lady became the country's leader in 1979.

THE THATCHER REVOLUTION AT WORK

The Iron Lady did not lose a moment before taking an axe to the welfare state which, in her opinion, only created dependence. Thatcher had her own vision of the social classes. According to her, the rifts that existed had to become a driver for the underprivileged classes: she deemed them necessary for people to be able to outdo themselves. She also led a campaign to weaken the trade unions, whose movements she regulated, notably with the 1982 law aimed at repressing aggressive strikes. In order to boost the economy, she gave people with high incomes a preferential tax rate: it decreased from 83% to 37%. Thatcherism had been definitively launched and would be very economically successful. However, it would take until 1990 for the record rate of inflation, 16%, to decrease by two thirds.

In 1983, the record of Thatcher's government was a disaster: production was falling, unemployment was rife and the public deficit was still rising. But as usual, the Iron Lady remained inflexible and refused to compromise. As she liked to repeat, there was no alternative.

FIGHTING FOR ARGENTINA

The Falklands War arrived at just the right moment, in 1982. On the one hand, the patriotic aspect of the battle would rally the British, and would enable Thatcher to be re-elected as Prime Minister for four years. On the other hand, the war would lead to disagreements within the Conservative Party. Several members of the government resigned to symbolically show their discontent.

365 DAYS OF STRIKES

The Second Thatcher Ministry decided to take on the mining sector. Noticing that around twenty mines were losing money, they decided to close them. This decision practically decimated jobs. A technically illegal strike then began, as only 40% of the miners decided to join it, while the law demanded a minimum of 55% for a strike to be declared legitimate. Despite the violent confrontations that took place between the police and the miners, the Iron Lady remained tenacious. Respect for the law came before anything else. Plans were put in place to avoid a coal shortage, and those who were not trade union members were enlisted to transport the ore.

Miners' protest in London, 1984.

From March 1984 to March 1985, Thatcher refused all of the compromises offered and opposed all negotiation attempts. Exhausted, in debt and hungry, the miners finally went back to work after a year of strike action, having obtained nothing from the government.

INTERNATIONAL AIMS

Following this came the privatisation of public businesses. Through this measure, Thatcher allowed the new owners to reduce the budget deficit and improved public finances at the same time. Additionally, the number of civil servants decreased and the government made drastic cuts in transport, healthcare and housing costs.

MORE NOTICEABLE SOCIAL INEQUALITY

The Thatcher government had barely had time to appreciate renewed growth when the trade deficit increased yet again.

THE TRADE DEFICIT

A country's trade deficit is calculated from an imaginary balance. If a country's imports are greater than its exports, it has what is known as a trade deficit, as it is dependent on another country for its goods.

The rate of unemployment was 5.8%, but social inequality continued to rise. The rich became even richer, and the poor became poorer. In this context, the Iron Lady tried to implement her Poll Tax. This would also affect the most underprivileged people who did not currently pay tax. She persevered, even when her colleagues told her that she was going too far, and ended up being ousted in favour of John Major (born 1943), who succeeded her in 1990.

HIGHLIGHTS

"I WANT MY MONEY BACK"

Thatcher truly made her mark during her first European summit in Dublin, on 30 November 1979. When the negotiations came to the subject of the budget, the Iron Lady made waves in the EEC (European Economic Community). Judging the United Kingdom's contributions to be too high, she announced to the assembly, "I want my money back." She in fact thought that her country gave much more than they received in return. Many people burst out laughing, and few believed that such a demand was possible. However, the nine member states (Germany, Belgium, France, the Netherlands, the United Kingdom, Luxembourg, Italy, Denmark and Ireland) spent almost the entire summit discussing Britain's rebate.

Although they were aware that the United Kingdom was one of the poorest countries in the EEC and its involvement was disproportionate, the other European countries blocked the Iron Lady's proposal. This was because changing the UK's contribution amount would involve changing the basic rules on which the Community had been founded. But they had forgotten about Thatcher's tenacity. After several interviews, she ended up convincing Valery Giscard d'Estaing (French statesman, born in 1926) and Helmut Kohl (German statesman, born in 1930) during the European summit at Fontainebleau in 1984. As proof, she had unfailingly demonstrated the minor importance of British agriculture (2% of GDP) compared with the giants of France and Germany.

This was therefore a total victory for Thatcher, who obtained a 66% rebate on the UK's contribution. The case of Britain was used as a point of reference, as one principle was made clear from it: any member state whose payments were too high in relation to its economic status could have its contribution revised and corrected.

"FAILURE IS NOT AN OPTION"

On 24 March 1976, Argentina underwent a coup d'état and came under a dictatorial regime. The situation was just as worrying in other South American countries, where an assassination campaign known as "Operation Condor" was being carried out by the secret services in order to eliminate political dissidents. The dictatorship thus spread to other countries, including the Falkland Islands on 2 April 1982. These islands had been under British rule since 1833.

A LONG-CONTESTED SOVEREIGNTY

The Falkland Islands are located in the Southern Atlantic, over 8000 miles away from the United Kingdom. They have not always belonged to the United Kingdom. In the 18th century, the French claimed them during their explorations, but were soon chased out by Spain. Spain decided to leave the Falkland Islands in 1810, bringing 37 years of occupation to an end. In 1820, Argentina was granted independence by Spain. Argentina saw this as their opportunity to establish a colony on the coveted islands, but this idea was quickly abandoned. The British then re-entered the fray by seizing the strategic location in 1833. Argentina and the United Kingdom have disputed the sovereignty of the territory ever since.

The United Nations put pressure on Argentina to withdraw its troops and stop occupying the islands with Resolution 502. But this was not enough for the Iron Lady; as well as achieving nothing, she was concerned that she would lose her glory and that her inaction would be perceived as cowardice. She therefore decided to react by launching an aggressive offensive against the occupiers of the Falklands on 25 April 1982. As well as the question of territory, several other factors were in play that might explain this somewhat unexpected reaction. The Falkland Islands were a strategic point due to their location, and more specifically their proximity to the Antarctic. It was therefore crucial to keep control of them in order to take advantage of the raw materials and exploitable riches around them. "Failure is not an option," stated Margaret Thatcher of the war she was then leading.

The battles, which were short but violent, led to the deaths of 650 Argentinians and 255 British soldiers. Once more, Thatcher was victorious, and her nationalist pride would be extremely attractive to voters in the 1983 elections. The Argentinian writer Jorge Luis Borges (1899-1986) would use a very specific simile to describe the war: "The Falklands thing was a fight between two bald men over a comb" (*The Guardian*, 2010).

"AND NOW IT MUST BE BUSINESS AS USUAL"

In Belfast (capital of Northern Ireland), the prison continued to fill up. Many members of the IRA (Irish Republican Army) were locked up there for their violent and reprehensible actions.

THE IRA

The IRA appeared in 1913 with the "Home Rule" project, whose main objective was gaining more autonomy for Ireland. It was not until six years later that the movement took on the name "IRA". It demanded the total independence of Ireland with violent attacks made against the British.

Throughout history, internal wars have consumed armies following differences of opinion as to which direction they should go. Out of such fights rose two IRAs, including the Provisional IRA who believed that using violence was necessary for achieving their aims. It would take until 1974 for this organisation to be officially deemed illegal, and 2005 for it to decide to abandon its use of weapons.

It was in 1976 that Bobby Sands and several other militants were arrested and sent to the Belfast prison. The imprisonment conditions were very harsh and particularly degrading. The detainees were beaten frequently and humiliated excessively. At the age of 22, the young Bobby

Sands did not let himself be pushed around. He became Officer Commanding of the IRA and had messages sent from inside the prison. He and his comrades fought for the status of political prisoners, in order to limit the mockery and end the violence committed towards them. While the British government turned a blind eye, the prisoners began the "Blanket protest", which involved refusing to wear their uniforms, preferring a sheet. But they did not see any improvement in their conditions. Bobby Sands therefore decided to reinforce the movement by launching a "no wash protest", or "dirty protest". The prisoners denied all forms of hygiene, refusing to wash themselves and even going as far as to smear their excrement on the walls. Staying true to her usual ways, the Iron Lady remained unmoved and barely even paid attention to these provocations. The detainees then began a hunger strike.

At the same time, in April 1981, when an IRA Member of Parliament died, the party members decided to suggest Bobby Sands, still in prison, to replace him. An election was thus organised, and the young rebel won, which would force the Thatcher government to change the law allowing prisoners to be elected.

After 66 days of relentless struggle, Bobby Sands died at the age of 27, taking his ideals of an independent Irish republic to the grave with him. The defeat was bitter. After 172 days, there had been ten deaths among those undertaking hunger strikes. The death toll was so high that the Iron Lady's cynicism and inflexibility caused many riots in Northern Ireland and led to great upheaval across the United Kingdom and beyond its borders. "He chose to take his own life," said Thatcher to justify herself, when public opinion held her responsible.

In 1984, the IRA tried to get its revenge by planting a bomb in the French hotel where the Prime Minister's party was holding a conference. Away from her room at the moment of the event, Thatcher only just avoided the attack which nonetheless took the lives of five Conservatives. Unfazed, the Iron Lady held her own by standing at the podium to make her speech, and said, "And now it must be business as usual."

A RELATIONSHIP THAT CHANGED HISTORY

Thatcher met Ronald Reagan, the governor of California, in London in 1975. More than love at first sight, they were truly political soulmates. Although they had their own specific qualities, the respective paths of these two people put them in power at almost the same time. Gradually, the two heads of state found things in common, particularly on account of their mutual enemy: communism. The Iron Lady did not seem to be afraid of anyone and used her eloquence to deal with any annoying questions. During a visit from Mikhail Gorbachev (Soviet statesman, born in 1931), she had no qualms about asking him why he did not allow his people to emigrate. Judging his confession to be a weakness, she could not help telling the story to her American friend. Thanks to the mutual influence they had on one another and to their determination, Reagan and Thatcher contributed to the fall of the Soviet Union.

Margaret Thatcher invited to the White House by Reagan, 1988.

THE SOVIET UNION

Also known as the USSR (Union of Soviet Socialist Republics), the Soviet Union was founded on 30 December 1922. It was made up of 15 Republics, which together formed a federal state. It owed its creation to the October Revolution of 1917, which ousted Tsar Nicolas II (1868-1918) and enabled the Bolshevik party to seize power. This unifying party was also, at the time, led by Lenin (Russian revolutionary and statesman, 1870-1924). In his desire to assemble everyone, Lenin organised his new Republics according to ethnic criteria. The management of these entities was entrusted to the only party in the USSR, the

Communist Party of the Soviet Union (CPSU).

Ronald Reagan and Margaret Thatcher got along extremely well. They had a very close relationship: he described her as "the best man in England", and she talked of him as though he was the second man in her life. Only minor disagreements, without any dramatic consequences, would oppose them, such as America's attempt to find a compromise during the Falklands War.

BETWEEN FONDNESS AND DIFFICULT COEXISTENCE

While Thatcher appeared to have the perfect political love affair with Reagan, her relationship with Queen Elizabeth II was more variable.

When Thatcher became Prime Minister, it was the first time a woman had obtained the position in the United Kingdom. Additionally, the Iron Lady was from a different background from that of the Queen, which did not stop her from following protocol to the letter, even though she allowed herself to use the 'royal we' when speaking, which had a way of annoying Elizabeth II, as this was a royal privilege. The Iron Lady's appearance and clothes also had worrying similarities with those of the Queen. Many people said this was due to a female rivalry issue.

The Queen's political views were rather centre-right, and she therefore approved Thatcher's severe economic reforms and the measures taken in the Falklands. However, their relationship became increasingly difficult when the Iron Lady refused any concessions during the miners' strike. Queen Elizabeth II found her too insensitive in the face of the miners' despair, and she had received many letters from their wives begging her to put an end to it. However, despite these disagreements, the Queen was fond of Thatcher. In 2007, she even helped her walk around a gala, holding her by the arm.

When Thatcher's death was announced, the Queen showed her sadness and her affection towards her. More surprising yet, Elizabeth II, despite being strongly attached to tradition, attended her funeral, a very rare event as the Queen had never been to a former Prime Minister's funeral, with the exception of Winston Churchill (1874-1965).

IMPACT

With her look, her well-tempered turns of phrase, her refusal of consensus and her ultraliberal politics, Thatcher certainly made an impact and profoundly changed the United Kingdom.

POLITICAL VOLUNTARISM

Although her decisions and opinions were always divisive, it cannot be denied that the Iron Lady had the spark and the devotion of political purpose. She was admired for her voluntarism and her reactions when faced with difficult situations. Even today, her attitude remains an example for the political class. On the other hand, her perception of politics is judged to have been too simplistic. Aware of her inflexibility, Thatcher clearly stated that, to her, "consensus seem[ed] to be the process of abandoning all beliefs, principles, values and policies." This phrase clearly sums up her passion and commitment towards her principles and values.

She was also the first woman in the United Kingdom to reach such a high political position. Mainly surrounded by men in her government, the Iron Lady always stayed away from discussions that were too 'feminine'. Although she rejected feminism, which she thought of as toxic, she nonetheless broke down many barriers for women, showing them that often the only ingredient for success is passion.

THE ECONOMY AT THE FOREFRONT

Thatcher undoubtedly contributed to the economic renewal of Great Britain by rewarding entrepreneurship and reducing the power of trade unions. By privatising public companies and deregulating finances, she gave more freedom to investors. The United Kingdom thus opened up to the international world and quickly attracted large amounts of foreign capital. Thanks to her, the City of London began to gain traction and became a major, globally recognised investment centre.

Her successors, including Tony Blair (born in 1953), never criticised her choices: they led their politics in the same direction. Despite the social crises, Thatcher enabled the United Kingdom to enjoy record prosperity from 1994 to 2008.

A WEAKENED STATE

One of Thatcher's main objectives was to considerably reduce the role of the state. Her wave of privatisation made the private sector the main driver of the British economy. But her many cuts in key sectors led to the disappearance of free healthcare and the loss of unemployment benefits for society's poorest. Society thus became divided into beneficiaries and outsiders. Immigration was also heavily affected by a whole series of measures.

Gradually, the state's role became minuscule. Its increasing lack of involvement in social matters led to an increase of inequality between the classes. In 1990, the income gap between the rich and the poor was at exactly the same level as it had been in 1930. And even today, the poorest 20% of society only earn a tiny percentage more than they did then. The income gap between classes remains one of the highest in an OECD (Organisation for Economic Co-operation and Development) country, with the United Kingdom 24th out of 28 countries.

THE END OF TRADE-UNION POWER

With her five laws on trade unions, Thatcher managed to lessen their role. She gave them a stricter way of working and introduced a sanction against aggressive strike action. Her indifference towards the miners' strike signalled the end of trade-union power over the country. Since then, the frequency of strikes has been considerably limited, as if the Iron Lady has successfully shattered the symbolism of trade-union action.

MARGARET THATCHER, A SOURCE OF INSPIRATION

Due to her political positions, her speeches and her attitude, the Iron Lady paradoxically established an excellent breeding ground for artistic creation. By getting rid of funding and reducing financial aid for culture, believing that artists had to prove themselves alone if they wanted to succeed, she attracted the rage of many of them. For her, contributing to art was out of the question, especially if that art was directed against her.

Her measures then inspired many musical groups of the time (The Smiths, The Clash, Morrissey, Madness, Elvis Costello and many others), who dedicated rather violent songs to her, thus demonstrating their way of responding to the oppression she imposed on the working classes. An anti-Thatcher movement was truly underway in British rock. The Iron Lady's political career also coincided with the appearance of a hedonistic movement featuring various wild parties during which people took large quantities of ecstasy: it was the emergence of rave culture.

But it was not only in the musical domain that Thatcher was a powerful subject of disagreements and debates. Cinema, painting, television, literature and even fashion were also influenced by the famous Iron Lady. As a general rule, plays, literature, paintings, television programmes and documentaries all took a fairly critical position towards Thatcher's work. And although when she died many heads of state paid homage to her, reactions were very different in the artistic domain, where aggressive criticism was once again launched. Ken Loach (British film and television producer, born in 1936), announced on the day she died, with at least a hint of irony, that her funeral should be privatised, which would have issued an invitation to tender and left the event to the highest bidder. In any case, the Iron Lady never left – and probably will never leave – people indifferent.

SUMMARY

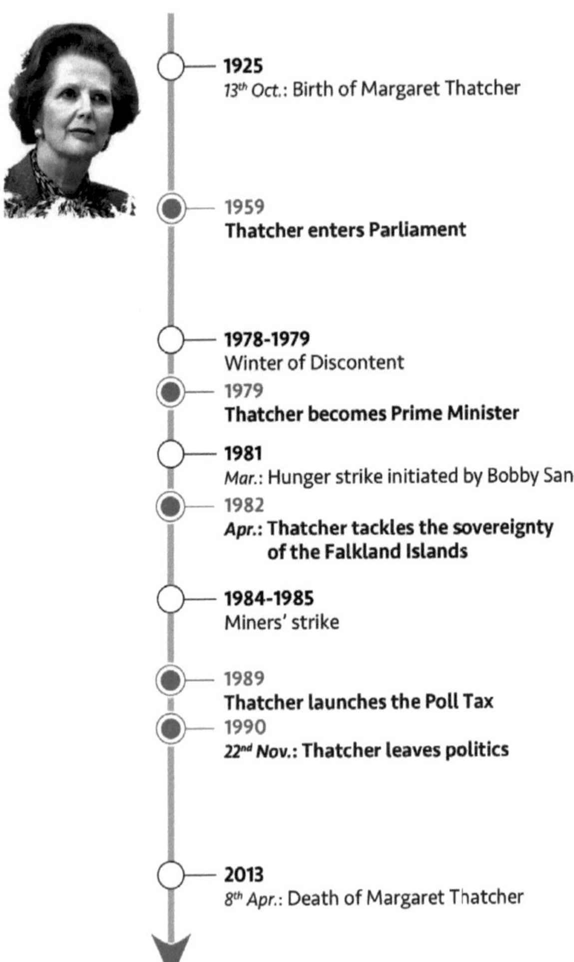

1925
13th Oct.: Birth of Margaret Thatcher

1959
Thatcher enters Parliament

1978-1979
Winter of Discontent

1979
Thatcher becomes Prime Minister

1981
Mar.: Hunger strike initiated by Bobby Sands

1982
Apr.: **Thatcher tackles the sovereignty
of the Falkland Islands**

1984-1985
Miners' strike

1989
Thatcher launches the Poll Tax

1990
22nd Nov.: **Thatcher leaves politics**

2013
8th Apr.: Death of Margaret Thatcher

- Born on 13 October 1925, Margaret Thatcher always adored her father, who gave her his Methodist values, a refusal to compromise, and rigour. She would keep these character traits throughout her political mandate and would also demonstrate them in her personal life.
- A leading political figure of the 20th century, she was not only the first female Prime Minister in the United Kingdom, but also the first in Europe, and the person who held the post for the longest. While her status as a woman was never particularly noteworthy, she proved that not being a man was not a handicap in the political jungle.
- In the collective mind-set, it was also her rhetoric and her retorts that were forever inimitable.
- A controversial figure on account of her economic policy, she took ultra-liberal, anti-trade union and Eurosceptic measures, while demonstrating an inflexible drive.
- Her policies enabled her to revitalise the British economy, attracting foreign investors and improving finances thanks to the large number of privatisations she undertook. In return, she drastically reduced the power of the state by making budget cuts notably in the health, transport, education and culture sectors. These measures unfortunately led to a rise in unemployment and an increased gap between the different social classes.
- Thatcher also helped to weaken the power of the trade unions at a time when strikes were extremely frequent. She was against socialism and the omnipotence of the British trade unions, which she considered to be internal enemies. She never gave in, despite the miners' struggle which lasted 365 days.

- The Falklands War, a brief but very deadly event, enabled her to win back the hearts of the electorate and be re-elected for a second term.
- She was a strong figure and inspired many artists in various domains, from painting to singing. As proof that she left nobody indifferent, an anti-Thatcher movement even developed in British rock. The Iron Lady also unintentionally contributed to the appearance of rave culture, which arrived in protest of her cuts to the culture budget.

FURTHER READING

BIBLIOGRAPHY

- Blagrove Jr, I. (no date) The Children of Thatcher and Reagan. *Rice N Peas.com*. [Online]. [Accessed 26 January 2015]. Available from: <http://www.ricenpeas.com/docs/the%20children%20of%20thatcher.html>
- Chabas, C. (2013) Margaret Thatcher : "L'adieu à dix millions de livres" qui fait hurler la presse. *Le Monde.fr*. [Online]. [Accessed 27 January 2015]. Available from: <http://www.lemonde.fr/europe/article/2013/04/11/margaretthatcher-l-adieu-a-dix-millions-de-livres-qui-fait-hurler-lapresse_3157596_3214.html>
- Colmant, P. (1979) À Dublin, face à ses partenaires européens, Mme Thatcher dénonce la situation "inique" de la Grande-Bretagne dans la CEE. *Le Soir*, 30 November 1979.
- Combes, F. (2013) Mort de Margaret Thatcher : un œillet rouge pour Bobby Sands. *L'Humanité.fr*. [Online]. [Accessed 20 January 2015]. Available from: <http://www.humanite.fr/mort-de-margaret-thatcher-un-oeillet-rouge-pour-bobby-sands>
- Compagnon, O. (no date) Guerre des Malouines. *Universalis.fr*. [Online]. [Accessed 28 January 2015]. Available from: <http://www.universalis.fr/encyclopedie/guerre-des-malouines/>
- Cullen, C. (1991) *Margaret Thatcher: Une dame de fer*. Paris: Odile Jacob.
- Czarni, R. (2014) En 1984, Margaret Thatcher a vu le coiffeur tous les trois jours (et autres histoires

- rendues publiques). *Slate.fr*. [Online]. [Accessed 28 January 2015]. Available from: <http://www.slate.fr/monde/81839/1984-margaret-thatcher-coiffeur-anec-dotes>
- Delmotte, A. (2003) *L'indispensable de la culture anglo-saxonne*. Levallois-Perret: Studyrama.
- De Visscher, C., Emery, J.-M. and Le Bussy, G. (2004) *La relation entre l'autorité politique et la haute administra-tion : mise en perspective de la situation au niveau fédéral en Belgique*. Ghent: Academia Press.
- Express.co.uk. *Ken Loach Blasts Plans For Margaret Thatcher's Costly Funeral*. [Online]. [Accessed 28 January 2015]. Available from: <http://www.express.co.uk/news/showbiz/390560/Ken-Loach-blasts-plans-for-Margaret-Thatcher-s-costly-funeral>
- Fontan, S. (2013) Bilan de Margaret Thatcher en Grande Bretagne. *L'Économiste.eu*. [Online]. [Accessed 28 January 2015]. Available from: <http://www.leconomiste.eu/decryptage-economie/12-bilanecono-mique-de-margaret-thatcher-en-grande-bretagne.html>
- Giulio Anta, C. (2007) *Les pères de l'Europe : sept portraits*. Brussels: Peter Lang.
- GQMagazine.fr. (2013) *Margaret Thatcher l'autre bilan*. [Online]. [Accessed 28 January 2015]. Available from: <http://www.gqmagazine.fr/pop-culture/medias/diaporama/margaret-thatcher-lautre-bilan/3893#1-elle-a-t-la-muse-dela-pop-anglaise>
- The Guardian (2010) *Falkland Islands: Imperial Pride*. [Online]. [Accessed 18 January 2015]. Available from: <http://www.theguardian.com/commentisfree/2010/feb/19/falkland-islands-editorial>

- Langelier, J.-P. (2013) Margaret Thatcher, portrait de la Dame de fer. *Le Monde.fr*. [Online]. [Accessed 9 January 2015]. Available from: <http://www.lemonde.fr/europe/article/2013/04/08/margaret-thatcher-la-dame-de-fer_1810460_3214.html>
- LeFigaro.fr (2013) *Thatcher : Mitterand a flatté sa féminité*. [Online]. [Accessed 10 January 2015]. Available from: <http://www.lefigaro.fr/flash-actu/2013/04/10/97001-20130410FILWWW01012-thatcher-mitterrand-avait-flatte-sa-feminite.php>
- Leinwand Leger, D. (2013) Thatcher, Reagan Relationship Altered History. *USA Today*. [Online]. [Accessed 26 January 2015]. Available from: <http://www.usatoday.com/story/news/world/2013/04/08/thatcher-reagan-political-soulmates/2063671/>
- Lévêque, E. (2013) Comment Margaret Thatcher a marqué l'économie et la société britannique. *Trends.be*. [Online]. [Accessed 27 January 2015]. Available from: <http://trends.levif.be/economie/people/comment-margaret-thatcher-a-marque-l-economie-et-la-societe-britannique/article-normal-215919.html>
- L'Express.fr. (2013) *Irlande du Nord : pas de regret pour Margaret Thatcher à Belfast-Ouest*. [Online]. [Accessed 23 January 2015]. Available from: <http://www.lexpress.fr/actualite/monde/l-irlande-du-nord-pas-de-regret-pour-margaret-thatcher-a-belfast-ouest_1240400.html>
- L'Express.fr. (2013) La Dame de fer en 10 dates clés. [Online]. [Accessed 12 January 2015]. Available from: <http://www.lexpress.fr/actualite/monde/europe/mort-de-margaret-thatcher-la-dame-de-fer-en-10-dates-cles_1238414.html>

- L'Express.fr. (2013) *Margaret Thatcher, tremplin malgré elle de la culture britannique.* [Online].[Accessed 28 January 2015]. Available from: <http://www.lexpress.fr/actualites/1/culture/margaret-thatcher-tremplin-malgre-elle-de-la-culture-britannique_1238516.html>
- L'internaute.com. *Qui est Élisabeth II ?* [Online]. [Accessed 27 January 2015]. Available from: <http://www.linternaute.com/actualite/interviews/07/marc-roche-elizabeth-2/3-elizabeth-2-premiers-ministres.shtml>
- Marzagalli, S. and Marnot, B. (2006) *Guerre et économie dans l'espace Atlantique du xvie au xxe siècle.* Pessac: Presses universitaires de Bordeaux.
- Mathieu, C. (2013) Élisabeth et Margaret la relation spéciale. *Parismatch.com.* [Online]. [Accessed 28 January 2015]. Available from: <http://www.parismatch.com/Royal-Blog/Royaume-Uni/La-reine-Elizabeth-et-Margaret-Thatcher-la-relation-speciale-507472>
- Nguyen, E. (2006) *100 événements du xxe siècle.* Levallois-Perret: Studyrama.
- OECD Data.org. *Royaume-Uni.* [Online]. [Accessed 28 January 2015]. Available from: <http://data.oecd.org/fr/royaume-uni.htm>
- Statistiques-mondiales.com. (no date) *Taux de chômage.* [Online]. [Accessed 28 January 2015]. Available from: <https://web.archive.org/web/20160810125839/http://www.statistiques-mondiales.com/chomage.htm>
- Supertino, G. (2013) Le "thatchérisme" pour les nuls. *Europe1.fr.* [Online]. [Accessed 20 January 2015]. Available from: <http://www.europe1.fr/economie/le-thatcherisme-pourles-nuls-1475411>

- Thatcher, M. (no date) Speech at Kensington Town Hall ("Britain Awake") 19 January 1976. *Margaret Thatcher Foundation.org*. [Online]. [Accessed 8 January 2015]. Available from: <http://www.margaretthatcher.org/speeches/displaydocument.asp?docid=102939>
- Thoraval, A. (2005) Le Royaume-Uni tient à sa "ristourne". *Libération.fr*. [Online]. [Accessed 15 January 2015]. Available from: <http://www.liberation.fr/evenement/2005/06/17/le-royaume-uni-tient-a-sa-ristourne_523726>
- Toupie.org. (no date) *Commonwealth*. [Online]. [Accessed 22 January 2015]. Available from: <http://www.toupie.org/Dictionnaire/Commonwealth.htm>
- Toupie.org. (no date) *État-providence*. [Online]. [Accessed 18 January 2015]. Available from: <http://www.toupie.org/Dictionnaire/Etat-providence.htm>

ICONOGRAPHIC SOURCES

- Portrait of Margaret Thatcher, dated 1983. © Rob Bogaerts.
- Photo of Margaret Thatcher in September 1975. © Library of Congress.
- Thatcher's coffin is taken to St. Paul's Cathedral, London. Royalty-free reproduction picture.
- Miners' protest in London, 1984. Royalty-free reproduction picture.
- Margaret Thatcher invited to the White House by Reagan, 1988. Royalty-free reproduction picture.